# It'

by Jane Simon

Printed in the United States of America

ISBN 0-15-313821-1

Ordering Options
ISBN 0-15-313991-9 (Grade 1 Collection)
ISBN 0-15-314033-X (package of 5)

2 3 4 5 6 7 8 9 10 026 99

I am hot.

1

I see the blue

pool

I see all of the  children .

3

I look up.

4

You see me go up.

I'm up on top!

I will go down.

I'm not hot!

TAKE-HOME BOOK
**Picture Perfect**
Use with "Sometimes."